Australia In Miniature Projects

Prison Rehabilitation
Detox
Community Service
Prisoner Opportunities
Reduced Recidivism
Resurrected Lives
Life Purpose

Rev. Mike Wanner

Table Of Contents

Introduction

Angel Raphael Speaks Volume 4 which was subtitled Angels, Alcoholics, Addicts, and Prisoners – On Yeah!. was written in 2016 as the latest book in a series of messages and healing books that started in 2013.

In "Chapter 20 – Wrap Up", I wrote
"Once upon a time. England had a great problem with prisoners like we do now. England banished them to a foreign land where these unwanted people created a great land of their own, and now the Queen visits them."

The term Australia In Miniature projects was introduced in the next book in the series *Angel Raphael Speaks Volume 5* which was subtitled *Prisoners Caring for Alcoholics - Australia In Miniature Projects Intro.*

That book went on to discuss the idea started in Volume 4 as it pertained to Prisoners caring for Alcoholics and was followed by Volume 6 which was about Prisoners Caring for Addicts.

Another book followed about the Contained Care Communities Concept and organizing to create possibilities for them. Now I get to explaining what is simple to Conceptualize but different in application because the circumstances are entirely different than the original event.

1 - Why I am Writing This Book

Messages of a call to healing and healing potential have been very intense for a long time, and I feel compelled to keep writing. Angel Raphael is again actively communicating, and the pieces of many things are coming together.

I was born in the cradle of liberty, Philadelphia, PA and did not fully understand all that until a White Buffalo experience in 2004. I served in the United States Air Force in Texas and Vietnam, and my life has been somewhat unique and exciting.

In the course of ministry, I see many examples of the importance of care and consideration. I am in no way an elitist as I talk to prisoners and prostitutes and drug addicts and all kinds of those with issues who think they are sane and some of the worst off who think they are not.

My goal is to accept everyone as they wish to be recognized. The creation of a Penal Colony in Australia was a Sea Change Event for England.

I never felt that England was particularly wise in that effort, but then I do not know the limitation of choices that they had back then, so I am not really in a position to judge.

The main event in my view is the big Questions –"Where Do We Go From Here." Of course, someday I would like to go back to Australia, but in the meantime, I would like to invite the authorities here to consider prisoners as candidates for Australia in Miniature Projects

2 - Acknowledging An Invitation

Three Years before Volume 4 of the Angel Raphael Speaks Series, Angel Raphael had invited me to visit prison energetically, and I did not respond as that was not something that I was delighted to hear. I avoided further thought about that concept.

Recently, I was brought to Addiction as a focus of my writing as I see so much of it during Pastoral Rounds at the Hospital.

Just before writing Volume Four, I completed a book called *Angels Are Always Around Addicts and Alcoholics* and I did not realize that the completion coincided with a news media production called Generation Addicted. The problem is enormous, but the answers are few.

Volume 4 provides a concept for consideration and some preliminary ideas to propose possibilities for addicts, alcoholics, and prisoners.

I have been as amazed about this as everyone reading my writings lately and find the whole process intriguing and a bit scary.

America relates best to freedom, and nothing here is forced except for realities which exist already. The hope is that many problems can be realigned during these trying times so that more quality of life is available to all the participants.

3 - Child Countries Of The Same Parent

While the History of America and Australia are different, our roots are the same. Like Australia, America served as a penal colony before the American Revolution

Now the progress of Australia has provided inspiration for me to share ideas that can conceptualize a revitalization of parts of American society based on the successes that Australia has accomplished.

I remember well my trip to the University of Sydney for a training sponsored by The Gendai Reiki Network Australia in 2007. We were all studying Gendai Reiki-ho with the founder Doi Sensei with translation by Hyakuten Inamoto. During the trip, I enjoyed the beauty and spirituality of the great nation.

In Australia, I felt very much at home because the people dynamics were very familiar as was the diversity of the people.

While in Sydney, I did Bridge Climb. As I stood on the top Girder of the Sydney Harbor Bridge in between the Flags of Australia and New South Wales, I looked down on the Archipelago and The Opera House and the fleet of tiny little looking Ocean Liners and Ferries. I never ever felt closer to God, and my gratitude was tremendous. I am still grateful for that particular moment of my life.

Reflecting right now on Australia reminds me that the freedom there and here is remarkable but the forefathers and foremothers there and here had their own struggles.

The messages in the Angel Raphael Speaks series have been tremendous. The concept of Australia In Miniature is quite vibrant as an image for Reinvigorating the lives of the previously convicted and incarcerated.

I really hope that this image can help show potential to those who are following the patterns of the past. Little things mean a lot.

When I went to Australia in 2007, I was greeted with questioning that I thought was strange because it was unfamiliar. I was asked if my shoes were clean and I stuttered because I did not understand the importance that the Australians knew about keeping their country free of elements that could endanger their quality of life.

If I had an opportunity today to ask every American if their minds were open, I would. I can so I will.

Dear Americans - Are your minds open to new ideas that can Free Many Citizens from Imprisonment?

4 - Concepts In Perpetual Evolution

Australia conveys the concept of freedom but it also carries the story of Freeing Prisoners to Start Over, and that is what I really would like American Jurisprudence to Consider.

It is my sincere hope that the idea of Contained Care Communities can help care for the Underserved. The Australia in Miniature image is one that I wish to use to generate little ideas about following in footsteps of the Australian people.

Australia is such a vibrant land which stands proudly among the nations of the world. I hope that their independence like American independence can shine like the sun to beckon People to the Clarity and Purpose of Democracy.

While in Australia, I was also impressed by their political struggles which were very different than the ones that I was familiar with but they were even personally like the ones that I see at home, and that makes sense because our parental history was similarly rooted in British Laws.

The Complexity of all the prison systems in America makes them almost impossible to describe in any moment in a comprehensive document as the whole group of systems are in perpetual momentum.

As things are brought up and discussed, the dynamics are already shifting, and that means more work, more shift, and more re-assessment. My plan is now being reset just to observe what is now and search for a direction of flow instead of an absolute answer.

A revelation that seems clear is to shortcut the process by minimizing pushing against what is and focusing on creating a possible relevant focus in the present towards the future. The good news is that will be easier for me to write.

The less than pleasant news will be that the reader needs to be much more active than they would probably like to be. I will be writing about the direction of where we are and you good people are invited to recheck the present as you read this and help develop possibilities for the future.

Yes, I invite you to every step of the process and evolution of this work. I apologize in advance as I will be taking more shortcuts than I would typically because as I encourage an earthquake of thinking, all the rules and realities and tense and concept will quiver. Buckle up for a roller coaster of thinking.

You may think I am a little reckless, but I think that is needed now. I want to stay in forwarding motion and skip the doting of some I's, and the crossing of some T's as the tedium of exact writing will undoubtedly cause me to miss the Train of Thought that is steaming along at high speed.

I apologize for any inconvenience this approach causes but the world I see is in chaos, and there is a need for a safety officer to rope off the hazards of now and the potholes going forward. I invite your participation in polishing the roughest phrases going forward by letting me know your polishing perspectives.

In order to streamline the thought process, You will notice a lot of segmenting and sharing content from other documents of mine and then some positioning for the present focus. This is necessary because I am trying to get across concepts with enough support so readers can comprehend without needing to read every previous book that I have written which may no longer apply as initially framed.

I almost stopped the flows of awareness that have been coming to me, but that does not bring me any peace of mind. I have asked for guidance, and the suggestion to me has been you.

While I need the expertise of those who have been interested enough to read this far, I also need to ask you to caution all your efforts in a Pro Bono effort for the Universe of the incarcerated. If your loved ones are part of the world of incarceration, they will benefit from universal efforts.

The world of incarceration includes all who are part of the effort, and I further invite you to see across the lines of position. The quality of life for Prisoners and Correction Officers are interrelated.

Each of them interacts with the individuals of the other community, but they also communicate with the group of their peers. The dynamics of the interactions vary.

There may be times when the individuals in one group can have empathy for the individuals on the other team. They may also have to watch their backs as not to seem to cross value lines of their own group and be at odds with the collective thought process.

5 - Sea Changes Can Happen Many Ways

Sea Change means different things to different people. To a mariner, a calm sea is a pleasant change after a hurricane.

To a merchant, seasons can bring positive or negative shifts in reality. For example, Christmas can produce an abundance of sales and profits.

Beautiful summer weather in winter can thrill seaside resorts. The same weather can bankrupt the ski chalets a few hundred miles away.

Your involvement with a particular member of the universe of incarceration is also impacted by very subtle things that do not affect others in the same way. This subtle variation is tremendously significant as a pivotal point in making changes.

I find it very difficult to read about the incarceration issues. I do not get all the subtleties that are represented by the words on the page even though I am reading to enhance my understanding.

Similarly, the ordinary men and women of the communities within the nations of the world also find it difficult to read about stories in the news about incarceration issues. You may notice that I use many words to describe prisons and incarceration and the subtle shift of the phrase can either simplify or complicate understanding.

I am giving examples of interest and understanding to incentivize you to think about these things in your pursuit of opportunities for changes in the systems that you are concerned within the communities where you or your loved ones are.

The creation of Australia as a penal colony was a Sea Change event targeted at solving problems in England. Sometimes, the speed at resolving issues can lead to less than adequate plans that are ill-suited to the results that are desired.

For England, solving the prisoner problems were supported with a logic of labor for agricultural projects to provide food. Management by decree and/or power pushiness is not always an efficient way to get things started.

Management success requires powerful information, can do leadership, motivation, spirit, and cooperation. You can read for yourself elsewhere that the early results in Australia could have had better planning and administration by England so that the success would have been more satisfying to the Crown.

Later in this writing, I will mention patience as an essential key to success in Prison Re-Invention that will benefit all within the universe of incarceration. The changes can also progressively help all those other citizens who can see more value from tax dollars that can be redirected from prison and be used to support other programs.

6 - Purpose

Each of us on the planet has different music that makes our toes tap and that state of awareness is worth the effort. This program can make no promises or guarantees of what can happen once purpose returns to anyone's life, but those who have loved ones in the universe of the incarcerated may have more opportunities within these concepts than elsewhere.

It is up to individuals to make their own decisions about the appropriateness of this program for themselves and those who they care about. It is also essential that participants give to the effort with the hope that someone may benefit and hopefully recognize that the someone may not be the ones they would choose individually but that the many who benefit from the collective changes may also include the one they would have wanted. The same person might not have benefited alone.

Giving without expectancy can be transformative. The purpose and the pride in participation can be significant to bring personal peace while one is waiting for changes to happen.

When one gives without expecting to receive, there is a balance within life that works on its' own license because giving and receiving are part of the same whole. Oneness with higher vibration raises the vibration of the one who made the difference.

The thinking is a conscious act that makes a difference. In the Bible from the <u>Book of Proverbs</u>, chapter 23, verse 7: "As a man thinketh in his heart so is he." Or she.

7 - "No Flies on You" Going Forward

This famous Australian Phrase says a lot about positivity as a separate course of action from what you see at the moment. Another tremendous anonymous quote is "Energy follows thought."

This quote shifts from the Book of proverbs thought in the last chapter and took your process from the past-present tense to the present-future tense.

You are where you have thought. You will be where you are thinking about how and where that will take you.

Angel Raphael Speaks in Message set nine said:
"Please consider as if the vibration of a prison existed on a scale that you could read called the love fear continuum. Consider that a single increment move on that line that went away from fear and moved towards love was actually beneficial to all who passed through the premises.

As you ever so slightly held that thought, you entertained the possibility for a shift for the imprisoned and guards of the future. Congratulations, for you, have allowed some light to shine on a subject that is almost perpetually locked in pessimism." ARS 9

This message openly talks about the complexity of the system, and when one is committed to a complex environment, then their existence is in a confusing state of being. That which is reasonable to those on the inside is not for those on the outside

I encourage all readers to speak to the world about the need for change and optimism. Intense fear vibrates to perpetuate fear and hold the intensity for those that view it. Extraordinary Optimism reverberates to preserve Blessings and keep the blessed energy for those that embrace it.

Invitation To A New Paradigm

Change can happen if it is two-sided. My view after following the messages that have been coming through me and the suggestions carried therein is that Change is a real possibility for those who wish to participate in it.

I believe that the Corrections Officers would like things to be different and I encourage them to think and pray about that. I think that those Jailed, and their families would like things to be different, and I encourage all of them (even those with life sentences) to think and pray about that.

The challenge is enormous, and I am grateful to be involved only with guided suggestions. Neither Angel Raphael or I can see any of the causes of resistance those involved in the incarceration universe may hold.

Soften please thy positions and identify all opportunities for many things to improve. A key may be to avoid blame and defensive positions and seek openness to the possibilities for respect and thanks.

8 - Respect Can Be an Unknown Power

When I invite respect, you may question - REALLY? Please indulge me ever so slightly.

Many people today are defensive about their rights and entitlements. Putting a rights chip and/or entitlements chip on your shoulder is ever so threatening to your power.

It is a challenge to those who need to prove themselves that here is a person who is willing to be challenged. While that is a real macho thing to do and may raise your image in some circles, it also is like playing with fire as it makes you vulnerable to people who might just ruin the quality of your life.

As I get older, I finally understand the wisdom that was shared when I was young and stupid. I wish I realized then what I know now. (It is probably not too late for you to listen to wise elders if you would like to be prudent and survive and thrive.)

Just to be clear, I was not really the most macho dude then and I am still not. My dad died when I was really young from Lung Cancer, and I was a real mess and had some real issues with authority and the actual prominent power, the guy named God.

I became acutely aware that cursing God out did not really help anything and other authorities were not good targets for my anger and hate either. I just wanted to understand why and I still crave that knowledge on a persistent basis.

It is easy for people to talk to me because they can tell that I want to help and that is an excellent step to getting along with people. I work well with spirit and energy. I know that each of us is still loved regardless of little deficiencies we see as significant.

I love diversity and the rainbow of skin colors and ancestries and of course the food variations they all share. Thank you, God, for all the people in my life and their problems too.

You may not have gotten my message yet about the power of respect, but I would really invite you to pursue it. The connection is key to the changes that so many would like to see.

If each reader can take a batch of respect and add detachment and then patience, real progress can be made toward recreating a Prison system that has all the attributes desired. The present methods have taken decades at least and some even centuries to become so involved and intertwined.

I invite you to start with respect, and I will present some exercise for you to begin to create a field of thought that can be fertile. Just like I have craved understanding, I know it can help all of you.

Detachment is also pivotal because so many folks focus on fault finding and blaming as a reason for the change. Not likely to be effective.

Patience is the next key because so many folks focus on impatience. Not likely to be effective.

9 - Unintentional Disrespect

{From Chapter 7 in *Surviving Hate And Vulnerability In America Now: The Power Is In You! By Me*}

Caution To Not Reject People You Do Not Know

The reactions between individuals are much more complicated than many may think. You may not know you are rejecting someone until you see their response to what you did not say.

The Gaze of Negativity

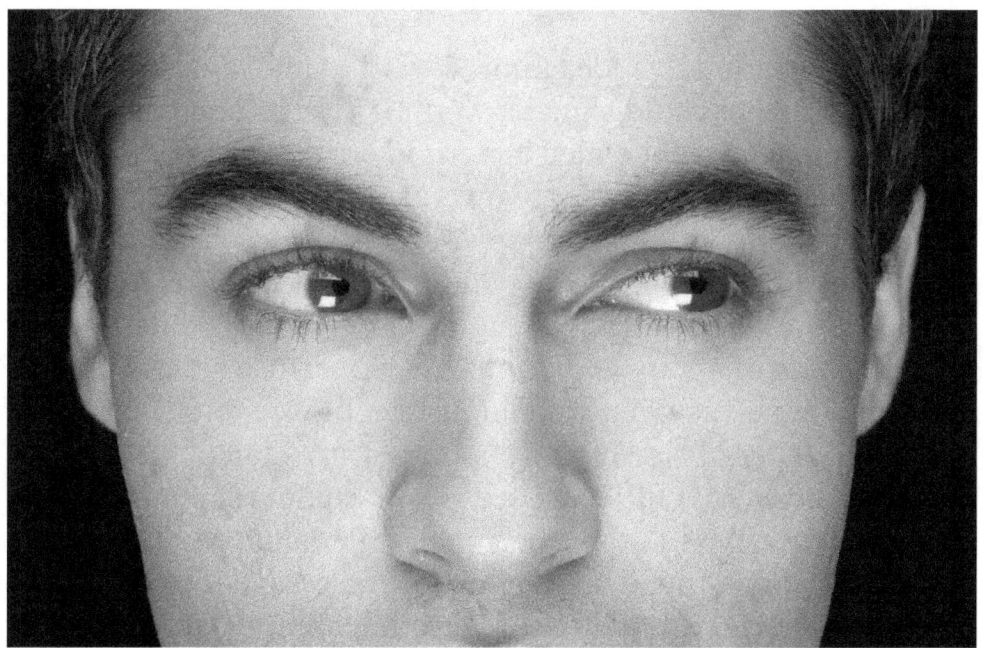

Consider a perspective I share that may not be defendable by scientific analysis but may be understood by those who try.

There can be a reactive triggering within people that can influence the outcome before a word is spoken.

How many times have you heard people say that as soon as they saw something, they knew this was going to be challenging, etc. Below the surface is a pattern of experience that can taint the energy between people that do not know each other and have not spoken a single word to one another.

I call it the gaze of rejection and being aware of it can help you to avoid damage to potential interactions when meeting new people.

I hope that sharing this idea allows us all to know our own vulnerability that could signal a warning for us. There is a psychological concept called pattern interrupts that could be implemented by those who are aware.

At the least, pattern interrupts could signal some of us to be on our best behavior during challenging times and good behavior can save a lot of agony and grief. We can diffuse situations by armoring ourselves with wisdom instead of weapons.

Please indulge me a little and see if you cannot remember a situation where you felt this personally. Perhaps, you were talking to a close friend about your last date, and your parent came into the room, and the conversation abruptly stopped.

You could have felt it, or your parents could have. Either way, the look hurts a lot whichever side of the issue you are on.

10 - Respect Exercises

I hope that you understood the subtlety of vulnerability above and that at a deep level you are able to create problems without even consciously trying. I want you to know that you may change that communication from negativity to positivity.

The way to change the subconscious mental communications is to improve the thoughts to positive ones so unconscious transmission will be set to help not hurt you.

To do that, you can choose to review how you think and reassess negative things. No, you do not have to, and you can perpetually attract the worst.

I include below an invitation to consider people in your life and reassess the level of respect that they may be worth.

It may be hard for you to understand that you have so much more power in your life than you thought. Even subtle perspective shifts can dramatically change the world outside your ears.

This can be very hard to comprehend, and there is no need or demand or requirement of any kind for you to take any action unless you really want change.

11 - Respect Finding

A free and independent resource to determine the truth about an individual is to learn how to dowse. A free course on how to do that can be found at http://LetterToRobin.org, and it is available in English, French, German, Italian, and Spanish.

Questions you might consider asking for a Yes/No response might be:

1. Am I reading this individual correctly?

2. Is something about this individual a trigger to me?

3. Is the individual a real threat to Me?

4. Is the individual neutral regarding me?

5. If I release my concern, will my energy and personal peace improve?

12 - Detachment

Detachment is also pivotal because so many folks focus on fault finding and blaming as a reason for the change. Not likely to be effective.

I invite you to own how you feel and take personal responsibility for it. You might just learn that it is far easier to change oneself from a belief that is not real than it is to convince somebody else that something you think erroneously is their fault.

None of us came with an instruction book, and many things have been programmed into the thinking of young people that is not the real truth. It can take some growing up to understand that many lies are presented as rules.

When you are attached to fighting over insignificant points of view that you and others hold as correct, there is no time left for analysis, reassessments, reality checks, research, and truth. The blame game that so many hide behind is a frustrating process that seeks pardon of the one who is blaming others.

Truth can surface when the distractions are removed, and objectivity can prevail. Pushing against what can become another distraction that can push reality further away.

There is excellent value in detachment and objectivity to convince the neutral observers that there is a depth of injustice that needs to be right whether or not the original cause and/or blame can be found. Detachment can allow expediency by keeping the goal in focus instead of obstacles to the target.

13 - Patience

Patience is another key because so many folks focus on pushing too hard while they are struggling against and the effort itself can cause resistance. Excellent sales people know that forcing people can be less convincing than patience and diligence.

You probably will not want another old expression from an old guy who did not want to hear old quotes either when he was younger. The reason that I persist in sharing stuff that you might not want is that many of you may need to know old wisdom because it contains the gems of perspective that can hold you in the embrace of readiness to receive a breakthrough in your thinking.

One old bit of anonymous wisdom is that "Rome was not Built in a Day" and you cannot change what is in a day either unless that day is the activation day of a plan, program, ideal, process of a breakthrough.

Prior to an activation day, there must be analysis, planning, deliberations, a master plan and the assemblage of all the players that are needed to do what needs to be done to recreate from the reality or what was into the version of a new story that contains the whole plan of what is to be.

You can help lead, participate, follow, fund, analyze, mastermind, coordinate and implement that plan if you want to. Do you want to?

If you answered yes, then put want to work.

14 - Summary

I hope that many can see that Sea Change has happened, can happen and may well happen again. This little book has carried a bit of thinking forward, and it has been limited because many can quit if the journey seems too long and not able to be accomplished.

This book may be a part of a guidebook that may never be completed, but the future does not have to be history before someone can contribute to furthering their society and their nation. Much of what is wrong in countries now just evolved with no one designing anything.

I am inviting you to participate in a future Sea Change that you can help design. There is excellent power in visionaries, and I encourage you to join in a new bright vision to realign freedom and justice for all.

This document is merely a suggestion for the development of a plan that can benefit many and that neither Angel Raphael or the author is a participant in any arrangement to provide any such service. A new program is needed to establish basic ideas, service concepts, cost concerns, responsibilities and some suggestions for services that align with the core of the plan.

These ideas are both simple and complex, and all participants at any level need to take full personal responsibility for their involvement.

With that being said, let us begin to develop some ideas that can form a foundation for the system that can be later finessed.

If there are 100 Australia in Miniature projects, there can be at least that many separate agreements for different groups as each plan could have special provisions in design and application of the arrangements for others. Furthermore, there could be many subset organizations that would be beneficial for other concerns.

This book is conceptually intertwined with others I have written and is still brief because of all of life is intertwined, and while we may get caught up in some limitations at times, that does not mean that we cannot separately design and implement new resources, techniques, and plans.

We are where our world has evolved to be. We have been to space and back. Now, let us help each other to understand the depth of our potential and achieve it so that we may assist all others to do the same. And in the process of understanding, let us find new ways.

I already have many new titles to consider writing, and I invite you to do the same. Our futures are limited only by our perspective. May all who read this be blessed and expand they're potential, so much more can be done, AND SO IT IS!

15 - How Can You Help

Australia in Miniature is a way to describe the possibilities for reinventing a segment of society in a Sea Change like dynamic. I would like to invite as many people as possible to participate in the process of re-inventing the prison system in a way that is focused on positive change and does not get mired in trying to blame people who made the only choices they could within a highly restricted legal system that was rooted in a medieval mentality of days long gone.

Please consider submitting ideas that can grow lives. Please see the next chapter and send suggestions and perspectives to me at ReverendMikeWanner@aol.com. Thoughtful design for change can enliven the prison process for those employed within it as well as those held in it. Job elimination is not a suggested goal but adding purpose, safety, possibilities, and efficiency are.

Please realize that I am over 70 already and you may need to be the one to establish your own series of plans. My role is merely to invite the good that change here can do for the whole nation or nations that step up and reassess.

Finances are tight in America, and there are many needs for national funding of programs that can enhance lives. Our social network could be improved dramatically and help to prevent many of the social and addiction issues that ravage the lives of our children and veterans and seniors.

Efficiency and fairness in the prisons can provide a lot more security than torturous prison terms and also provide a foundation for prisoners to get out and stay out of jail.

16 - Perspective Invitation

I invite every reader to consider submitting a simple 200-word article about an idea that has the capability to be the seed of a positive perspective shift for the readers of it in the arena of prison reinvention. This is not an invitation to vent or blame.

This is an invitation to share something wise that can be the seed that is needed by those who read your seed. You could intend that they will be able to focus their energy in a way that will prepare for the fruit of your idea seed to blossom and help them and others.

The messages could help heal, release, grow from, process, understand, rethink, conceptualize, organize and otherwise analyze the who, what, when, where, how and why of an event. Understanding things can allow new perspectives on the ways that everything and everyone fit into the grand scheme of things.

Life is an experience, and it has a timeline for us all. While you are here, you can celebrate so much that what you are observing dissipates. Such is the way of all who are addicted to any measure of substance or pleasure in a solo experience.

There is nothing wrong with seeking joy. A high path to pleasure is while others are also experiencing a benefit as that will usually extend your enjoyment as you participate in their happiness.

{Page Configuration - <220 Words, 6 x9, .5 margins, Title 20 Pt. Times New Roman, Body 14 Pt. Times New Roman}

For
Considering
These
Ideas

18 - Resource List

Distant Healing Sessions (or Join Mail List) – Write To mikewann@voicenet.com

Books by Rev. Mike at www.Amazon.com

Veterans Healing Six Pack
1. *Trauma Healing Options for VA Hospitals: Help for Veterans to Own Their Healing and their future.*
2. *Trauma Healing Action Steps for Veterans: Help to Start Healing*
3. *Trauma Healing Action Steps for Veterans: Empowerment*
4. *Trauma Healing Action Steps for Veterans: Forgiveness*
5. *Trauma Healing Action Steps for Veterans: Thought Freedom*
6. *Tea For Veterans: Welcome One Home*

PTSD Power Pack:
1. *The PTSD Project: Turn Pain To Power*
2. *PTSD & Soul Retrieval: Putting One Back Together*
3. *PTSD & The Purple PAD: Calling all Scientists and PTSD Patients*

Angel Raphael Speaks Volume 1: Take Courage! God Has Healing in Store for You!
Angel Raphael Speaks Volume 2: Take Courage! God Has Healing in Store for You!
Angel Raphael Speaks Volume 3: Take Courage! God Has Healing in Store for You!
Angel Raphael Speaks Volume 4: Angels, Addicts, Alcoholics & Prisoners – Oh Yeah!
Angel Raphael Speaks Volume 5: Prisoners Caring for Alcoholics - Australia In Miniature Projects Intro
Angel Raphael Speaks Volume 6: Prisoners Caring for Addicts - Australia In Miniature For Addicts
Reiki Journaling from Japan
Reiki Is Alive: God's Great Gift
Four Parts to Healing

Distant Healing: We Are All Connected
Stress Release Energy Work: How To Cope
Does Reiki Love Heal Cancer?
Group Consciousness
Salute To Philadelphia VA Medical Center: Thank You
Reiki Transcript for Reiki 2 & 3 Channels: Dr. Usui Is That You?
God Bless Kindle & Amazon
Puppies Are Different From People
If Your Dog Dies
Toy Guns Are Obsolete
Great Spirit Made Children With Red Skin: AND
The Cage of Fear: Is Not Locked
God Made Children Red, Yellow, Brown, Black & White: Greet Each Child With Kindness
Emergency Medical Kindness In The Cradle Of Liberty: Big City – Cracked Bell
Angels Are Always Around Addicts and Addicts: Help Is Near Now! Invite It In!
Angels Are Always Around Addicts and Alcoholics: Volume 2 - Tools To Help Re-Light Your Life
Prison Jobs Now: Providing Care For Addicts And Addicts
Controlled Care Communities Concept

Little Books on Kindle.com by Rev. Mike:
English Medical History Questionnaire For Non-English Speakers
English Language Helper For Non-English Speakers
Wise Wonderful Women Are The Well Of The Family
Answers for Tests & Research: Dowsing Power
Crisis? Reiki! Baby? Reiki!
Bible References For Healing
Angel Raphael Speaks – Prisons
Angel Raphael Speaks – Veterans
The Saint Off Interstate 95

Angel Raphael Speaks through Rev. Mike Wanner. Please visit
http://www.AngelRaphaelSpeaks.com

19 - Private Channeling

Angel Raphael Speaks a series of free messages that are channeled through Reverend Mike Wanner for the Highest good and Highest Healing of all concerned.

Many questions arise about Reverend Mike doing private channeling, and he does help with that so e-mail him.

Reverend Mike is available worldwide as a psychic channel, emotional release facilitator, spiritual energy practitioner & teacher, and public speaker. He looks forward to meeting you soon!

Email - mikewann@voicenet.com 215-342-1270
PRIVATE SPIRITUAL READINGS/channelings or Spiritual Healing Sessions: Telephone or in person.

Rev. Mike is available for individual, intuitive one-on-one sessions with you, his Guide Family, and your Guides. He helps by offering clarity on emotional situations about your life, your purpose, your spirituality, and the release of stuffed emotions
and cellular memory.
> Connect to the love of your Guides today!
> Contact Rev. Mike for an appointment.

Sessions available:

Spiritual Readings	Angel Channeling
Distant Reiki Healing	Distant Clearing of Stuffed Emotions
Distant Clearing Cellular Memory	Distant Clearing Energy Blockages
Distant Clearing of the Chakras	Customized needs

Mastermind dowsing responses to yes/no direction finding questions.

Rev. Mike is a facilitator of healing. He brings you and the Divine together so that you can align with the Divine and have a great time and a great life. All healing is between you and God, as it should be. Go ahead and start without Rev. Mike. Visit his prayer site http://www.Create-A-Prayer.com. Take the first step NOW.

20 - Reverend Mike Wanner

Rev. Mike Wanner started his metaphysical and ministerial studies with Reiki in 1993 and had studied seven styles of Reiki in the U.S., Japan, Canada, Denmark and Australia. He is certified to teach. He became certified to teach Integrated Energy Therapy in 1999 and co-taught the first IET class of the new Millennium. Mike began dowsing in 2001.

Ordained as a Metaphysical Minister of the International Metaphysical Ministry and an Interfaith Minister of the Circle of Miracles Ministry, Rev. Mike practices and teaches spiritual energy therapies in the Philadelphia Area.

Rev. Mike holds ministerial degrees from the University of Metaphysics and the University of Sedona. He is a Pastoral Care Associate of Aria – Frankford Hospital. He taught at the National Academy of Massage Therapy and Health Sciences.

Rev. Mike was a faculty member of the Medical Mission Sister's Center for Human Integration's School of Integrated Body/Mind Therapies in Fox Chase, Philadelphia, PA for twelve years.

Rev. Mike is licensed by the teaching of Intuitional Metaphysics to practice Spiritual Healing and Scientific Prayer. Mike is also a Prayer therapist.

Rev. Mike was elected in 2007 to the status of "Fellow of the American Institute of Stress."

In 2008, Rev. Mike became a practitioner of Coincidental Recognition as he incorporated the CoRe system into his spiritual healing practice.

In 2009, Rev. Mike trademarked a new healing process called Quantum Quatro! Subtle Energy System Support®.
In 2011, Rev. Mike joined the outreach program known as the Health Advantage Group.

In 2012, Rev. Mike became a Certified Professional Coach by The Master Coaching Academy and Joined The Personal Empowerment Group.

Prior to his metaphysical, ministerial and coaching studies, Rev. Mike worked for Sears Roebuck and Co. while in High School and after graduation, until he joined the U. S. Air Force in 1965. He returned to Sears from Vietnam in 1969 and stayed until 1978. His final Sears assignment was as an efficiency expert in Methods - Operational Research and Development.

He volunteered with Burholme Emergency Medical Services from 1969 and is still a Life Member and Board of Directors Member. He started a private ambulance company in 1975 and worked professionally in the field until 2001 when he devoted his full attention to real estate investing, healing, coaching, and writing.

www.ReverendMikeWanner.com

www.ingramcontent.com/pod-product-compliance
Lightning Source LLC
Chambersburg PA
CBHW070728180526
45167CB00004B/1664